The Publishers wish to thank Betty Nelson, A.R.A.D.,
editorial advisor, for her valuable help in ensuring
the correctness of this edition.

Published in 1992 by
Hamlyn Children's Books,
part of Reed International Books Ltd.,
Michelin House, 81 Fulham Road,
London SW3 6RB

Original edition published in French under
the title of "Mes premiers pas de danse classique"

300 rue Léon-Joulin 31101 Toulouse – France

ISBN 0 600 57653 1

Printed in Belgium

MARIE-LAURE MEDOVA

First Steps in BALLET

HAMLYN

1

Your first steps

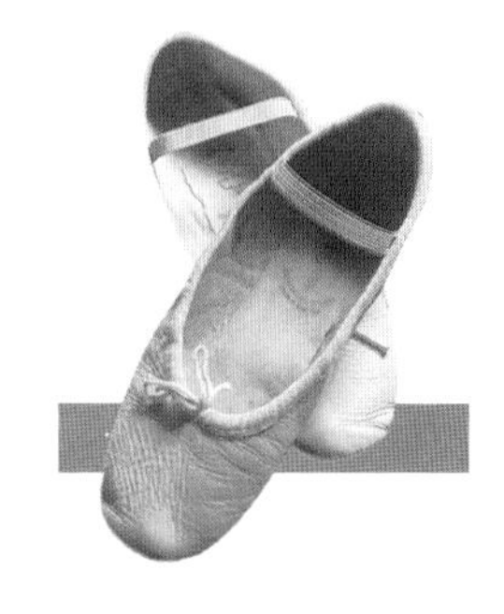

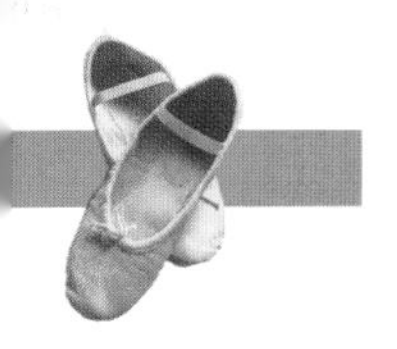

At what age can you start?

You can start to learn ballet from the age of 7, and perhaps even a little earlier. Your teacher will be able to tell you whether you are ready or not.

The teacher will adapt the lesson to the age of her pupils.

What happens in a ballet class?

A ballet class usually lasts for one hour. You start by warming up: you stretch to make your muscles more supple and to prepare them for harder work to come. First of all you may do some floor exercises, then you will work at the barre. You will warm up with some pliés; then bit by bit you will work your whole body. The barre helps you to keep your balance – you will learn to hold yourself correctly there.

You will then move on to exercises in the centre of the room, but they are a little more difficult as you don't have the barre to help you any more. It's up to you to find your balance. It is through the work in the centre that you will learn to move gracefully. The teacher will move about during the class to correct you, or to give you advice or to explain a movement that you haven't understood.

The ballet studio

The floor of the ballet studio is made of sprung wood: it allows you to jump and land without jarring your spine. On the walls there are mirrors, which are very important: you have to watch yourself to be able to correct bad positioning. Along the walls, two barres act as a support for certain exercises. All the exercises take place to music, since rhythm is the base of dance. The only time you can chat with your friends is while you are getting changed before and after the class. During the class – ssh! Only the teacher is allowed to speak.

Two barres to lean on and a mirror to correct your positioning.

What do you wear?

For girls: a leotard, white tights and pale pink elasticated ballet shoes.
For boys: a white T-shirt, black tights and black elasticated ballet shoes.
Your hair must not get in the way. If it is long, tie it up in a bun. It is important to have a neat appearance at all times.

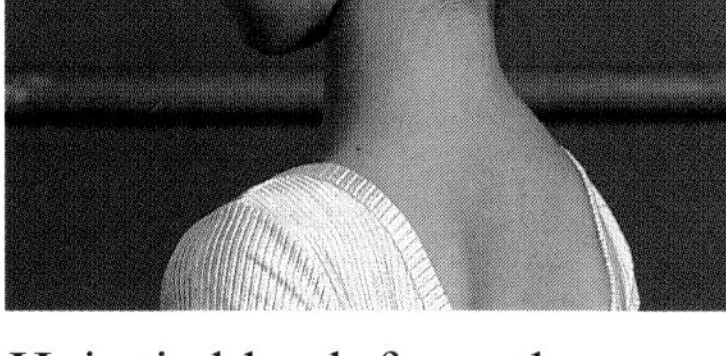

Hair tied back from the nape of the neck gives a lovely line.

Ballet shoes are sold without elastic. They have to have elastic sewn into them as shown in the photograph, to hold them on.

No pointe shoes yet. You will need many years of training before you are ready to wear them.

The ballet class

To start with you will learn to walk gracefully, to run lightly, and to listen to the rhythms of the music. Then will come the exercises on the floor, at the barre and in the centre of the room. But first of all you must learn the 'five positions'.

The five positions

Without the five positions, you could not learn a single movement. In fact almost all ballet steps start and finish with one of these.
For each position of the feet there is a matching position of the arms. The pictures show young pupils learning the five positions.

First position

The arms are lifted and gently rounded. The legs are straight. The heels are touching, and the feet are well turned out.

Second position

The arms are opened and lightly rounded. The feet are apart and still well turned out.

Third position

The right arm is brought up into a half-circle while the left arm stays in second position. The heel of the right foot is placed against the middle of the left foot.

Fourth position

The right arm remains in the vertical position and the left is brought forwards into first position. The right foot slides forward to lie parallel to the left foot. The space between them should be the length of one foot.

Fifth position

The arms are brought above the head to form a curve. The hands are not touching. The two feet are close together so that the toes of each foot are touching the heel of the other.

Floor exercises

Floor exercises help you to gain suppleness in various joints. They can strengthen your back, stomach and leg muscles.
Only practice them with your teachers help.

Increasing the suppleness in your back and strengthening your stomach muscles

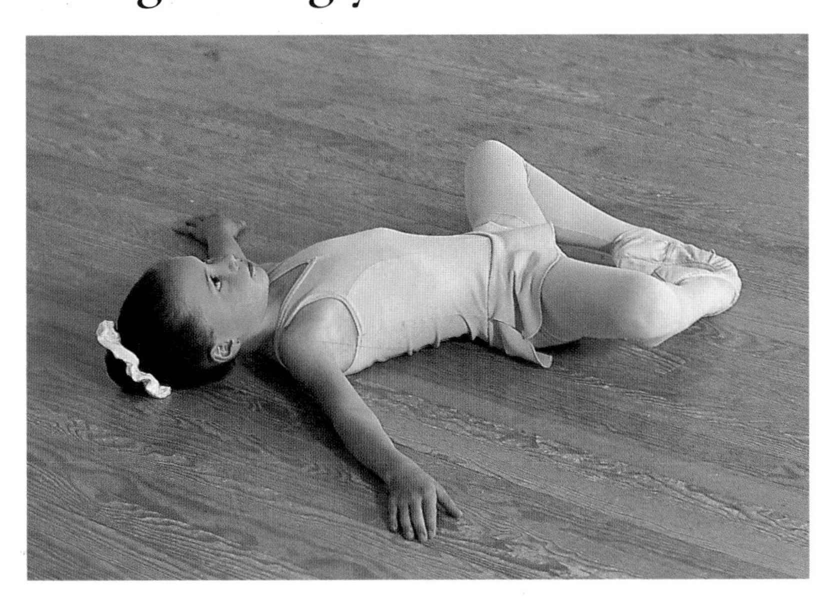

1 Lie flat on the floor. Spread your arms to the side and bend your legs. The pointed toes should be touching and the heels just apart.

2 Sit up keeping your knees open and your feet together. The arms are in fifth position, and your back should be perfectly straight.

3 Your teacher can help you to lean forwards keeping your back flat and straight.

4 Finish the movement by relaxing your back and leaning forwards as low to the ground as possible.

5 Bring yourself back up to sitting position, with a flat back and arms rounded in fifth position.

6 Keeping your back straight, bring your arms down to first position. Repeat the exercise slowly sinking back towards the floor, keeping your back rounded, to return to the starting position (1 or 4).

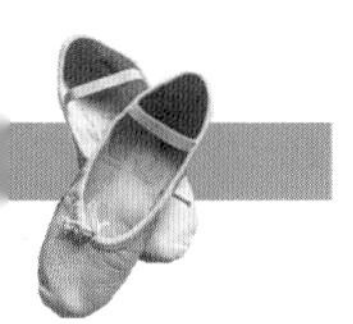

Raising the legs and stretching the thighs

1 Lie flat on the floor with one straight leg crossed over the other, pointing the toes to the ground.

2 Lift your right leg – it must be perfectly straight.

3 Pass the straightened leg to the side without touching the floor. Your back and pelvis should remain flat against the floor.

4 Return to the starting point, brushing the floor with your straightened leg.

5 Bring the same leg up, letting the foot glide up the calf to the knee. Your hips should stay flat on the floor. The heel of the bent leg is not touching the other leg.

6 Bring the leg down and cross it over the other leg returning to the starting position.

As you must exercise both legs – all that remains is for you to start the exercise again on the other side.

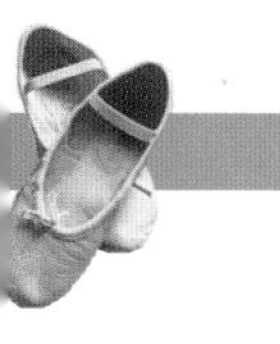

Stretching the thighs

1 Sit with your legs bent, pointed toes together and heels apart. Raise and lower the knees towards the floor.

2 Straighten out your legs, toes pointed towards the floor, and stretch them out sideways as low as possible. Bend them again, and return to the starting position.

Stretching the sides

1 Sit on the floor and open your legs as wide as possible. Raise your arms to fifth position, keeping your back flat.

2 Bring your left arm down while twisting towards your left leg.

3 Lower your chest over the leg. Your right arm should be parallel to your leg. Your left arm is in second position. Gradually come back up to the starting position, and repeat on the right hand side.

Positioning the hips

1 Sit on the floor and bend your legs with the soles of your feet together. Straighten your back. Place your hands behind you and lean back on them.

2 Take your right heel in your right hand, then straighten the leg in front of you, keeping your back straight.

3 Pass the straightened leg to the side, with your back still upright.

4 Release your hand keeping your leg perfectly straight.

5 Return to the starting position, and repeat the exercise with the other leg.

The barre

Work at the barre prepares for the exercises in the centre, and later for real ballet performances. The barre helps you to find your balance more easily. All the exercises should be practised on one side, then on the other, to make sure you work both sides of your body equally.

Pliés in first position

1 Stand sideways at the barre, your feet and free arm in first position.

2 Open your arm into second position.

3 With your heels touching, bend your knees keeping the heels on the floor – this is called a demi-plié.

4 For a grand plié, bend your knees completely, raising your heels from the floor as you do so. Lower your free arm to the starting position.

5 Rise slowly, passing through the demi-plié. Raise your arm to first position.

6 Open your arm to second position.

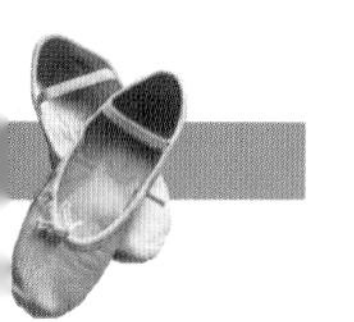

Relevé facing the barre

1 Demi-plié in first position, keeping your ankles and back straight, and your shoulders down.

2 Then straighten your legs.

3 Relevé onto demi-pointe with your heels forward.

4 Lower to first position without bending your knees, and repeat the movement again from the beginning.

Relevé in sixth position

1 Stand facing the barre with your legs straight and your feet together, keeping your back perfectly straight.

2 Rise to demi-pointe lifting your heels as high as possible.

Port de bras with cambré

1 Stand in fifth position. Slowly bend as low as possible to try and touch your chest to your legs, then . . .

2 . . . return to the upright position gently arching backwards, your arm stretched out and your head turned to the extended arm.

Balancing at the knee

1 With the supporting leg on demi-pointe, place your pointed foot at the knee. Your free arm is in third position.

Second and arabesque

1 High second: your supporting leg must be perfectly straight. Raise the other leg – which is straightened and well turned out. Your back must remain upright, with your arm in third position.

2 Arabesque facing the barre – an arabesque is a movement which is performed very slowly. Your back is as straight as possible, and your head upright.

Foot on the barre

1 Place your foot on the barre in open fourth position on demi-pointe.

2 Take your foot in your hand.

The splits

1 The splits is the last exercise at the barre. After a full warm-up, the teacher helps the pupil, who holds onto the barre, to raise her leg higher than she could do by herself. **But be careful! This exercise should only be done with the teacher's help.**

2 Side splits. The length of both legs should be touching the floor.

3 The splits.

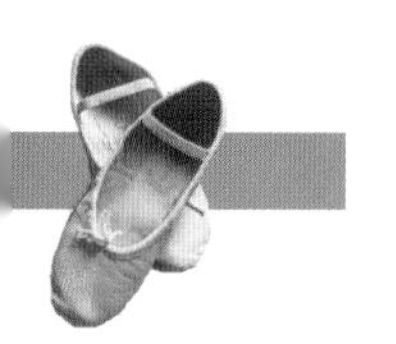

The centre

After the barre, you will move into the centre of the studio where there is no support. You have only your own sense of balance to rely on. After a few exercises, you will learn some simple routines.

The port de bras

The work of the arms in ballet is very important. In a performance you speak with your hands and arms. You will learn to move them gracefully.

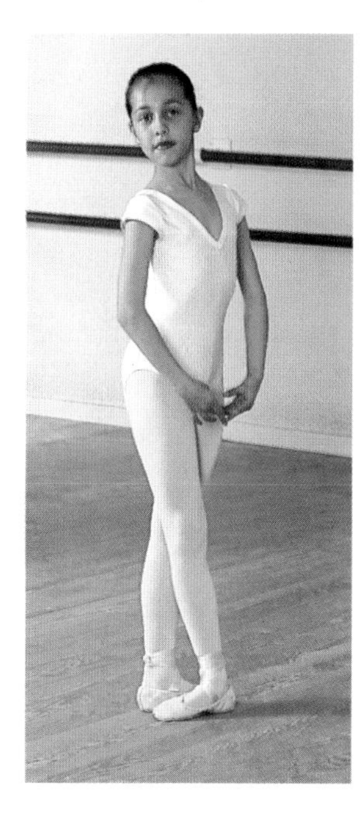

1 Stand in fifth position with your shoulders back.

2 Raise your arms to first position.

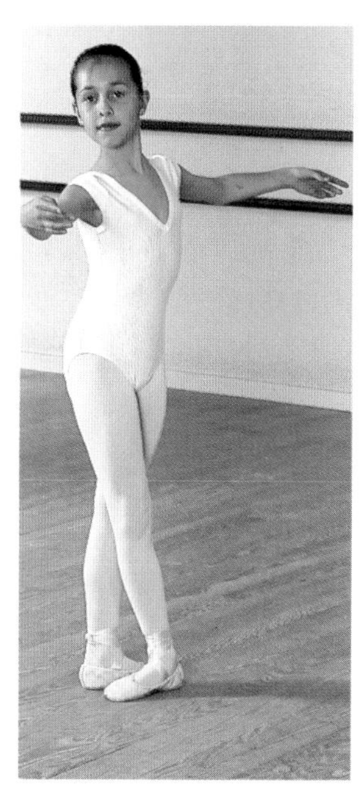

3 Then open them to second.

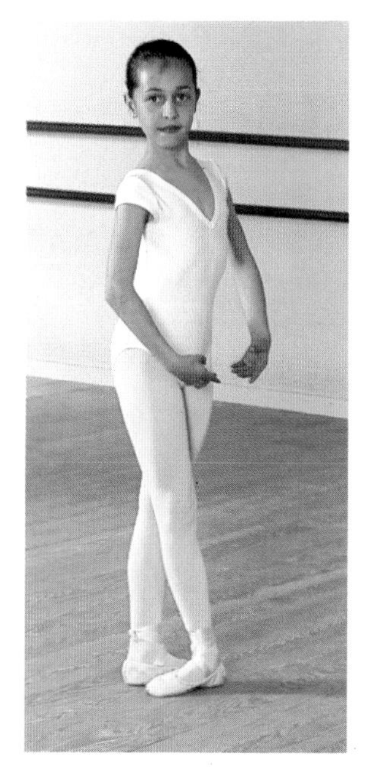

4 Return to fifth position.

5 Raise your arms again to first.

6 Then into third position. Don't forget to follow the movement of your arm with your head.

7 Lower your right arm to second . . .

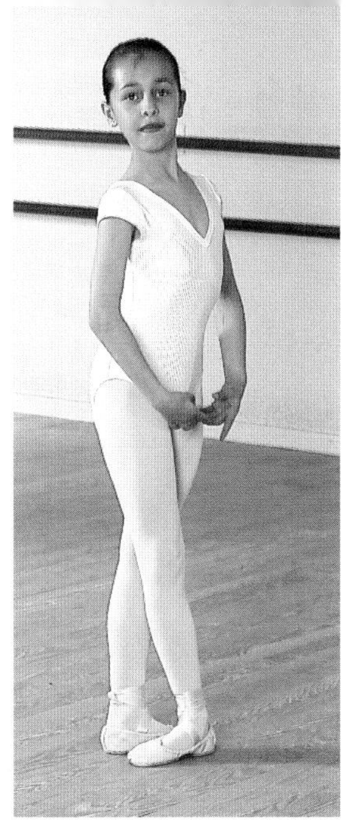

8 . . . then bring both arms back to the starting position.

9 Bring your arms back to first position . . .

10 . . . then raise them into fifth position.

11 Bring them down to second.

12 Return to fifth position. Change the position of your feet to repeat the exercise.

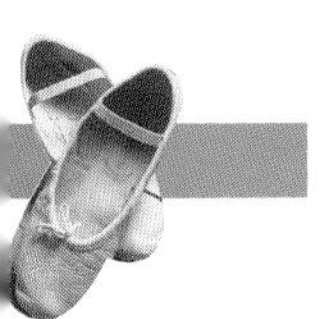

The pas de bourrée

1 Stand in the centre of the room in fifth position, with your right foot behind and your arms in the starting position.

2 Bend your legs and bring your arms up to first position. Keep your back straight.

3 Place your right leg in second, holding it slightly off the floor and pointing the toe.

4 Rise to demi-pointe with straight legs.

5 Staying on demi-pointe, move your front leg into second. Open your arms to second position.

6 Bring your right leg back in front of your left, in a demi-plié and lower your arms.

7 To finish the pas de bourrée, straighten your legs and return to fifth position.

Échappé épaulé

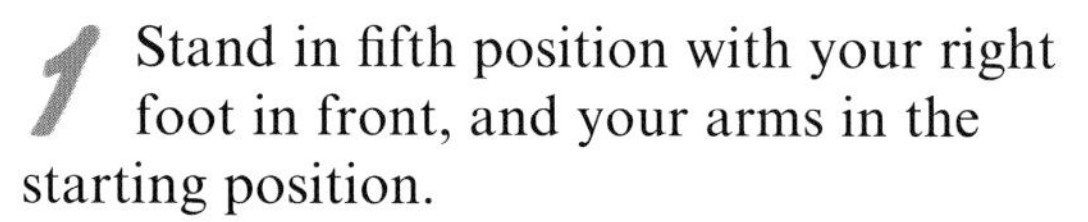

1 Stand in fifth position with your right foot in front, and your arms in the starting position.

2 Bend your legs and bring your arms up into first position.

3 Rise into second on demi-pointe and open your arms to second position.

4 Bring your feet back to fifth with the left foot passing in front, and both legs bent.

5 Repeat your échappé in the other direction.

6 Then bring your feet back to fifth position, with the right foot back in front.

7 Finish by straightening your legs and placing your arms in the starting position.

Relevé to the knee

1 Stand in fifth position with the right leg in front and your arms in sixth position.

2 Bend your legs.

3 Relevé onto demi-pointe and place the front leg at the knee. Then lower, bending your legs, and finish by straightening your legs as at the beginning.

Arabesque

An arabesque is a very difficult movement, as you must have an excellent sense of balance.

1 Balance on one leg. Bring the other leg up, straight, behind you – half way to start with . . .

2 . . . then all the way up.

3 An arabesque on demi-pointe with the help of the teacher.

Pointe work

Who has not dreamed of dancing on pointes, and looking like those elegant ballerinas who hardly seem to touch the floor? But be careful, you should wait until you are at least 10 or 12 before you start pointe work.

Exercise No.1

1 Face the barre in second position. Keep your feet well turned out.

2 Without bending your knees, rise to demi-pointe. . . .

3 Then on to pointe, keeping your shoulders down and turn your heels towards the barre.

4 Stay on pointe, keep the feet turned out, and plie in second.

5 Lower yourself to demi-pointe. . . .

6 . . . and onto the floor, keeping your ankles strong and back straight.

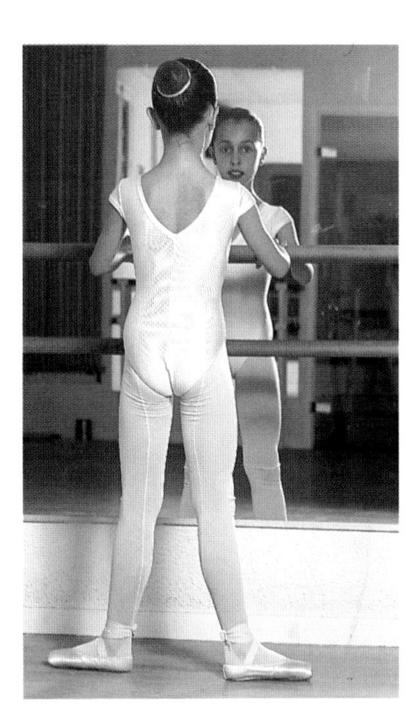

7 Straighten your legs to return to second.

8 Rise to pointe, find your balance, and repeat the exercise several times.

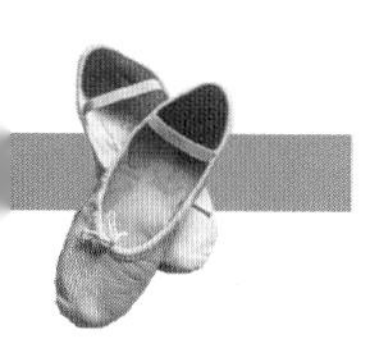

Exercise No.2

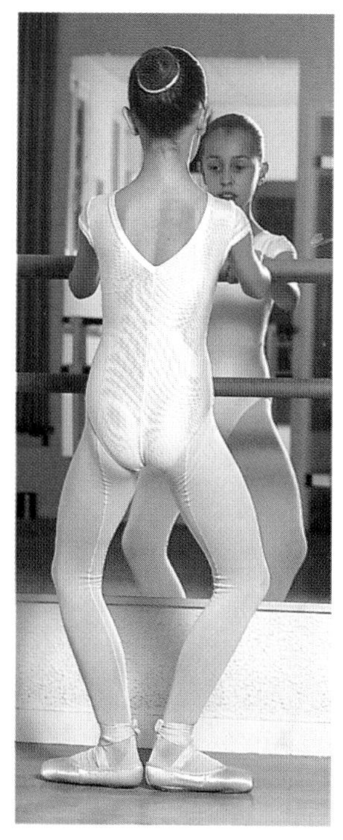

1 Demi-plié in first position.

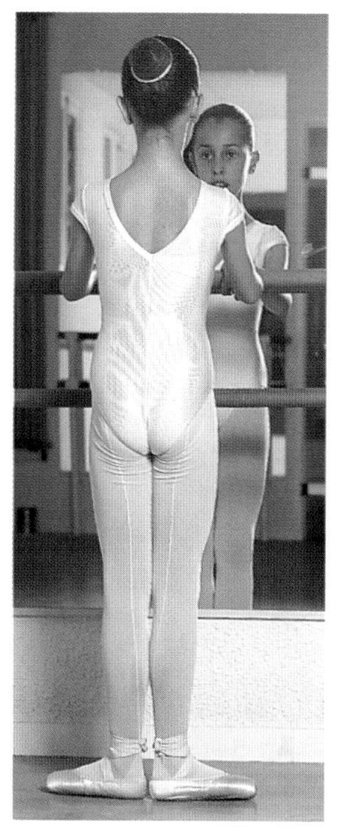

2 Straighten your legs.

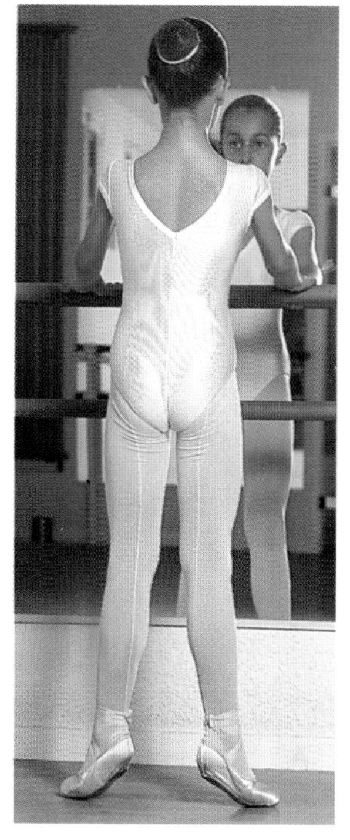

3 Rise to demi-pointe without bending your knees.

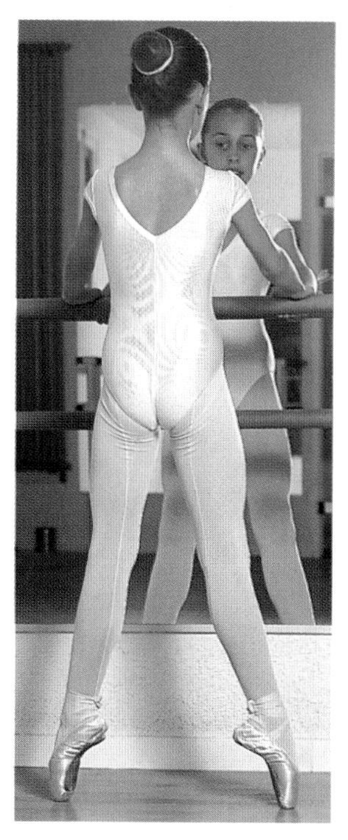

4 Rise to pointe.

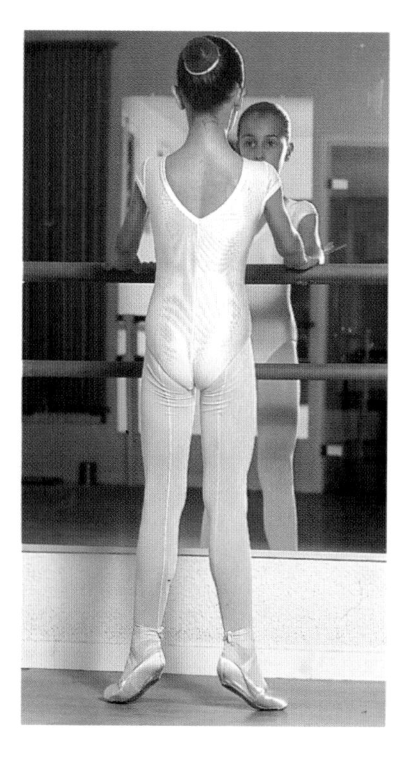

5 Lower to demi-pointe.

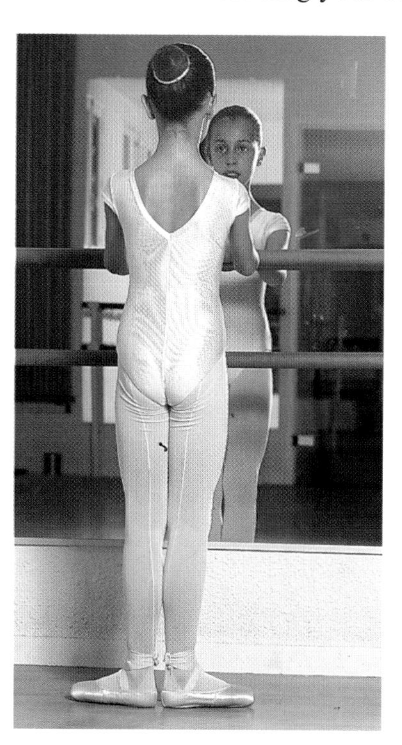

6 . . . and lower your heels.

7 Finish on pointe.

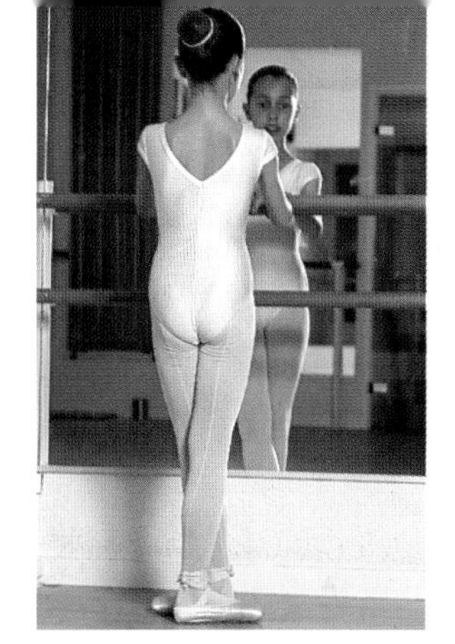

Échappés followed by a relevé in fifth position

1 Face the barre in fifth position beginning with your left foot in front.

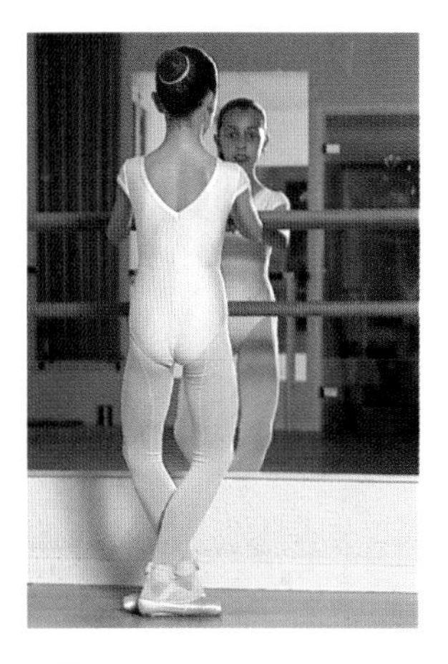

2 Bend your legs.

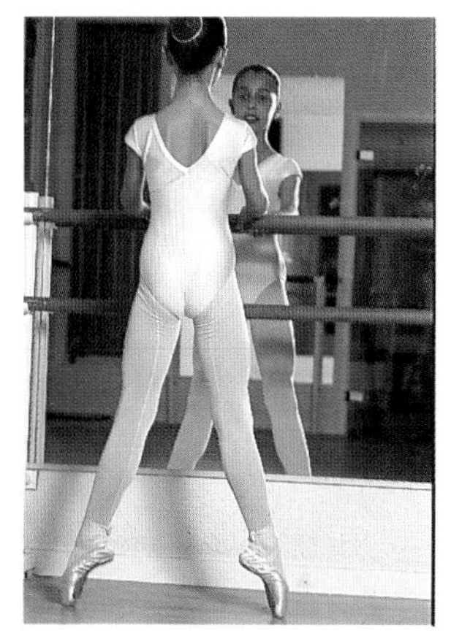

3 Then rise to pointe in second position, with your legs straight.

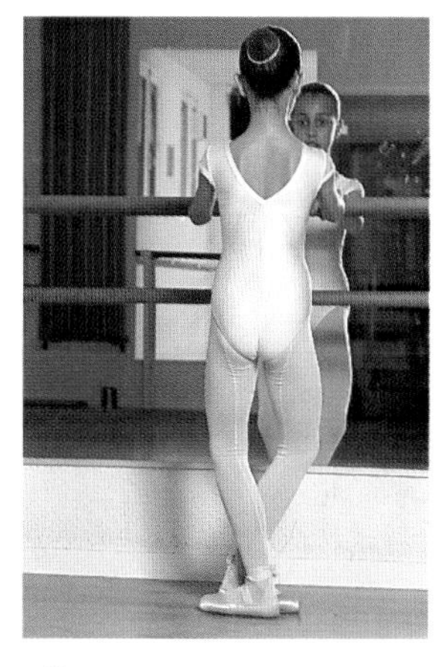

4 Lower into fifth in a demi-plié, having changed feet – your right foot is now in front.

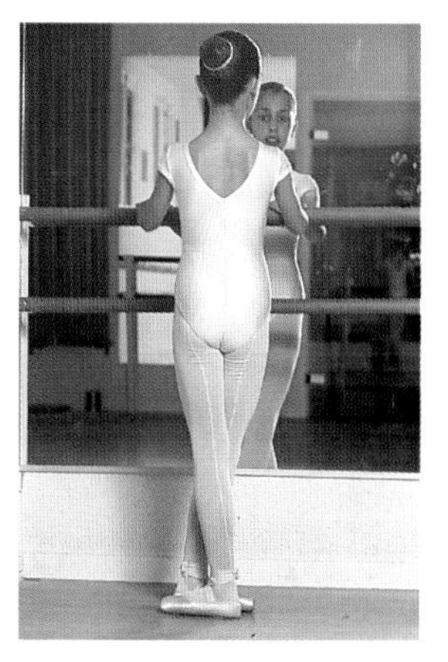

5 Straighten your legs.

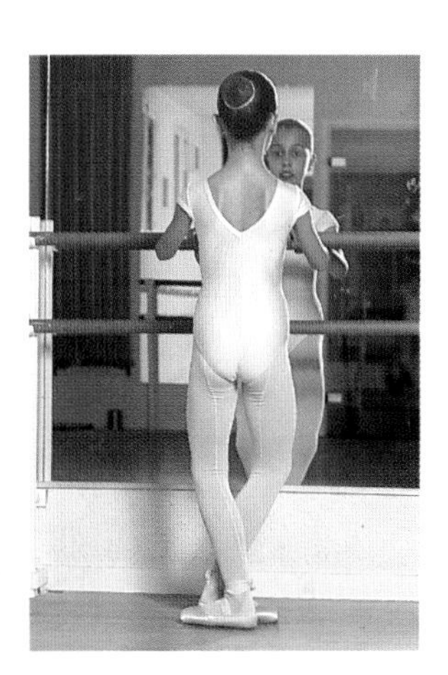

6 Bend your legs once more.

7 Rise to pointe keeping your feet tightly crossed, one foot in front of the other.

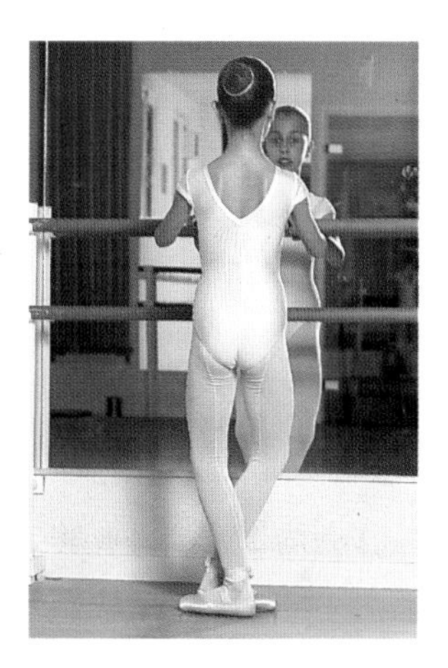

8 Lower into a demi-plié in fifth.

9 To finish straighten your legs. You can now repeat the exercise with the other leg.

JARDIN

3

And now for the stage

Have you rehearsed enough?
Are you sure you know your routine?
Because the big day is near . . .
You are going to dance on the stage
in a real theatre, in costume,
in front of an audience.
The work in class has a single goal –
to prepare you to take your place in a real ballet.
Even the greatest dancers spend several hours
every day warming-up and rehearsing.

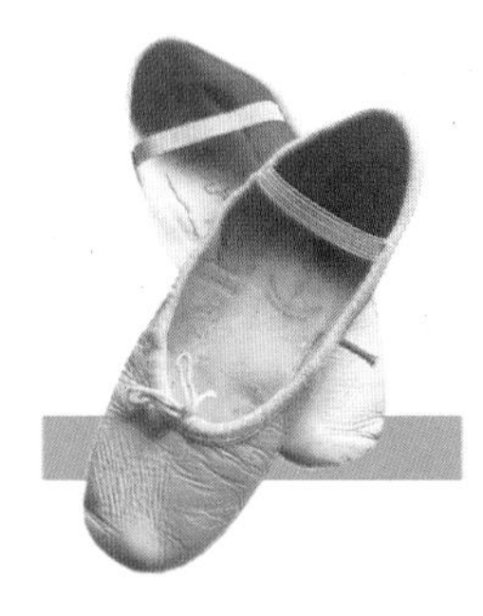

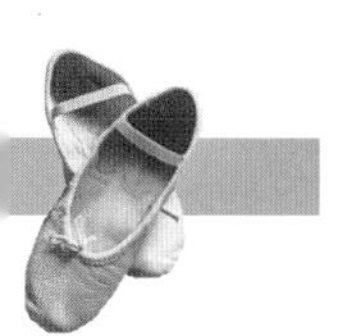

On the day of the performance you must be ready. One mistake and you threaten the success of the whole ballet. So you must know your steps very well, and also know how to dance along with the others. You will see, the long hours of rehearsal won't have been wasted.

The curtain rises and all you think of is dancing!

A ballet is above all a way of telling a story. This story has to be presented on the stage, and it's the choreographer who does this – he invents routines, series of movements, which the dancers have to learn and follow exactly. Of course, this all takes place to the rhythms of the music.
Are you ready?
Well, forget your stage fright, and dance!

▲
On the day of the performance there is no room for improvisation.

▲
Make-up will emphasise your features.

▲
Costumes and props are part of the performance.

Lighting shows the set off to its full advantage.
▼

The choreographer perfects the movements and the dancers' steps.
▼

With the participation of Amandine, Celia, Eleonore, Fanny, Florence and Sophie, Florence, Laetitia, Marie-Odile, Maud, Sophie.
The photos were taken at the Academie de Danse Classique Marie-Laure MEDOVA; 18–18BIS, rue Agathoise in Toulouse.
Thanks to VICARD who kindly provided the dance wear.

Photos: Edition Milan and Augustin de Berranger for pages 40 and 41.

Contents